VIENNA

TRAVEL GUIDE 2024

Explore Vienna's Undiscovered Gems:
An Insider's Handbook to the City's
Sounds, Sights and Tastes

Andrea J. Armstrong

TABLE OF CONTENT

CHAPTER 1

INTRODUCTION

Welcome to Vienna

 Alesha had always wanted to travel to Vienna, a city renowned for its ageless elegance and depth of cultural diversity. Her trip to this historic Austrian capital was more than simply a vacation; it was an opportunity to fully immerse herself in the past and present of Europe, as this city had for centuries been a hotbed of artistic and intellectual activity. With every minute that went by as her jet dropped approaching Vienna International Airport, Alesha's enthusiasm increased. The expansive vistas, abundant vegetation, and the gently flowing Danube River provided a charming first impression of the city. She had

been waiting for this moment her entire life, and the excitement was tangible.

As soon as Alesha left the airport, she experienced Vienna's allure for the first time. With a sense of nostalgia, the cool fall air seemed to carry the murmurs of two of the most renowned sons of the city, Mozart and Beethoven. There was always the possibility of musical delight, and Alesha was eager to learn more about the rich musical history of the city.

Her lodging was a charming boutique hotel tucked away in the middle of a maze of Gothic and Baroque structures in Vienna. Alesha went through Vienna's Old Town, the historic Innere Stadt, feeling as though she had entered a storybook. She followed cobblestone streets to St. Stephen's Cathedral, a magnificent example of Gothic architecture that rose high into the sky. She felt as though she had traveled through time because of the breathtaking architecture and sense of history all about her.

Of course, Vienna was more than simply a pretty picture. Alesha's investigation of the city of art brought her to the Kunsthistorisches Museum, where she was astounded by the creations of illustrious artists. The walls were covered in paintings by famous artists like Raphael and Titian, whose brushstrokes told a tale of human experience across time. Alesha was moved by the level of inventiveness that was on exhibit.

But Vienna was more than simply art and history it was a living, breathing city. Alesha was drawn to the vibrant outdoor market, Naschmarkt, by its wide selection of exotic foods, spices, and fresh fruit. She discovered herself enjoying Sachertorte, Wiener schnitzel, and other regional specialties while taking in the varied gastronomic landscape of the city.

For Alesha, coffee culture in Vienna was another new experience. She took a seat in a classic coffee shop, had a slice of apple strudel, and sipped delicious coffee. She was able to genuinely enjoy the city's love of the simple pleasures in life and the art of conversation because of the relaxed atmosphere and slow pace of the café.

Alesha's footsteps took her into Schönbrunn Palace's enchanted gardens as the sun began to set. Vienna's imperial past was preserved at the palace, which was a tribute to its grandeur and history. The exquisitely lighted gardens offered a calm environment in which to reflect on the city's timeless allure and its capacity to unite the old and the new.

Alesha had an incredible trip to Vienna, a sensory extravaganza that gave her a deep respect for the city's singular fusion of culture, history, and modernity. She had never had a more amazing encounter that left her with priceless memories and a lifelong bond with this fascinating treasure of Europe. Alesha saw Vienna as a realization of his dreams, and the city had lived up to its image as a city of dreams.

10 Reasons to Visit Vienna

Ten compelling and intriguing reasons to visit Vienna

Historical Magnificence: Vienna, the former capital of the Habsburg Empire, has a long and rich past. Discover the city's imperial heritage by touring historic locations including St. Stephen's Cathedral, Hofburg Palace, and Schönbrunn Palace.

Majestic Palaces: Some of Europe's most exquisite palaces can be found in Vienna. Apart from Schönbrunn and Hofburg, you may explore the Imperial Palace and Belvedere Palace, each possessing an own architectural allure.

World-Class Museums: The Kunsthistorisches Museum, Albertina, and the Museum of Natural History are just a few of Vienna's many outstanding museums. Art lovers will discover an abundance of magnificent works.

Musical Heritage: Vienna is regarded as the "City of Music" and is home to classical music superstars like Beethoven, Strauss, and Mozart. To experience the rich musical history of the city, go to the House of Music or catch a classical concert.

Coffee Culture: Vienna is famous for its coffee house culture. Savor a slice of Sachertorte, unwind in a classic café, and take in the distinct atmosphere that has long served as an inspiration to authors and thinkers.

Danube River: The Danube River winds through Vienna and provides lovely paths for bicycling, boating, and strolling. In the center of the city, Danube Island is a recreational haven that you should not miss.

Viennese Cuisine: Taste delicious Austrian cuisine, such as Sachertorte, Apfelstrudel, and Wiener Schnitzel. A delicious blend of modern and traditional cuisines may be found in the city's culinary scene.

Green Spaces: Vienna boasts an abundance of parks and gardens, making it one of the greenest cities globally. In the middle of the city, there are quiet retreats like Schönbrunn Gardens, Stadtpark, and Prater Park.

Markets with a vibrant atmosphere: Take a tour of Vienna's humming markets, like the Naschmarkt, which sells fresh vegetables, foreign food, and antiques. It is a great location to experience local culture firsthand.

Christmas Markets: Vienna's Christmas markets are a lovely experience to be had during the winter. Squares throughout the city come alive with holiday cheer, music, and delectable food.

Brief History and Culture of Vienna

Austria's capital, Vienna, is a living example of how history and cultural development have changed throughout time. Vienna's history stretches back to the Roman era and is marked by artistic excellence, intellectual enlightenment, and imperial grandeur.

Historical Tapestry

The Habsburg dynasty, a family that shaped Vienna for more than six centuries, is interspersed throughout the city's history. The Habsburg Empire, one of the most powerful states in Europe, was at the center of this control. Vienna's role as the imperial capital influenced the city's culture and architectural style.

Schönbrunn Palace is one of Vienna's most recognizable historical attractions. The expansive gardens and palatial interiors of this magnificent Baroque castle, which was home to the Habsburgs, provide an insight into the emperors' rich lifestyles. The Imperial Apartments and the Sisi Museum, which honors Austria's Empress Elisabeth, are two of the many palaces and museums that make up the Hofburg Palace, another jewel in the Habsburg crown.

Vienna was also a major hub for European art and intellectual history. Prominent intellectuals like Sigmund Freud and Ludwig Wittgenstein gathered in the city, which aided in the advancement of philosophy and psychology. The radical art movement known as the Vienna Secession first appeared in the late 1800s and had a profound effect on the development of the city's cultural scene.

Cultural Treasures

Vienna has a rich and varied cultural legacy. The music culture in the city is legendary. Mozart, Beethoven, and Strauss were born there, and their music is still heard in opera houses and concert halls today. Vienna is home to many concerts and events including classical music, and the city is well-known for its world-class productions of the Vienna State Opera.

The café culture of Vienna is also well-known. The city's café culture is centuries old and has long served as a hub for intellectuals, writers, and artists. A cup of coffee and a slice of Sachertorte can be enjoyed in a distinctive setting at classic coffee shops like Café Central and Café Sperl.

Vienna's museums hold a wealth of historical and artistic treasures. The Albertina Museum features a wide selection of graphic art, and the Kunsthistorisches Museum has an outstanding collection of artworks. A cultural complex with exhibitions, modern art, and a lively environment is the MuseumsQuartier.

The capital of Austria is also home to some amazing architectural designs. An architectural wonder, St. Stephen's Cathedral is distinguished by its colorful, multicolored ceiling tiles. Vienna's skyline is given a modern touch by the city's modern architecture, which is exemplified by the majestic Danube Tower and the landmark Hundertwasserhaus.

Geography and Climate

Vienna's geographic location combines urban elegance with natural beauty. The magnificent Danube River, undulating hills, and a mild continental climate with distinct seasons all year round characterize the city's topography.

Geography

Vienna is situated on the borders of the Czech Republic, Slovakia, and Hungary in the northeastern region of the country. One of Europe's principal rivers, the Danube, runs parallel to the city's shores and meanders elegantly through the urban landscape. The river enhances Vienna's recreational options in addition to its aesthetic appeal.

The topography of the city is made up of a mixture of plains, undulating hills, and hillsides covered with vineyards. To the west, the Vienna Woods (Wienerwald) give a verdant, wooded backdrop to the city as well as a plethora of chances for bicycling, hiking, and nature appreciation.

Vienna's metropolitan region is divided into multiple districts, and the city's center is situated across the Danube River and connected by a bridge network. On the right bank are historic neighborhoods like Innere Stadt and Leopoldstadt, and on the left bank are neighborhoods like Mariahilf and Neubau.

Climate

Vienna has a continental climate that is moderate with distinct seasons all year long. A summary of the city's climate is as follows

Spring (March to May): Gardens are in flower and the weather in Vienna starts to warm up progressively. It's a great time to take advantage of the nice weather and see the city's outdoor attractions.

Summer (June to August): Vienna experiences warm, frequently sunny summers. Daytime temperatures are perfect for outdoor activities, park picnics, and al fresco eating because they can reach the mid-20s to low 30s degrees Celsius (mid-70s to low 90s degrees Fahrenheit).

Autumn (September to November): With its pleasant temperatures and vibrant foliage in the Vienna Woods, autumn is a great season to visit Vienna. Cultural events abound as the city's parks and gardens take on a golden tint.

Winter (December to February): December through February is a chilly, frequently snowy season. Even though the city experiences below freezing temperatures, many enjoy visiting it in the winter because of its charming Christmas markets and joyous mood. The city's old structures and streets take on a mystical quality when snow is a possibility.

Vienna has a temperate climate all year round, with somewhat drier summers and heavier precipitation in the spring and fall. The city is attractive to tourists year-round due to its comparatively high amount of sunshine hours.

Arriving Vienna

By Air
Vienna International Airport is a classy way to meet the efficiency and attractiveness of the Austrian city. The biggest

and busiest airport in Austria, Flughafen Wien-Schwechat, provides a quick and easy way to arrive in Vienna.

Vienna's scenic surroundings are visible outside your window as your jet descends toward it. The distinctive spires of St. Stephen's Cathedral, the rolling hills, and the meandering Danube River offer a breathtaking introduction to your stay.

When you disembark, you find yourself in a contemporary, orderly terminal where the fusion of old and new is readily visible. Vienna greets you with immaculate cleanliness, unambiguous signs, and an air of efficiency.

There is good access to the city core from the Vienna Airport. In just 16 minutes, the City Airport Train (CAT) will whisk you straight to the Wien Mitte railway station in the center of Vienna, making it a quick and pleasant choice. As an alternative, there are several bus routes and the suburban rail (S-Bahn) that offer affordable transportation options.

The processes for passport control and customs are usually simple and effective, making for a hassle free trip. Retrieving bags is quick and finding information and services about transportation in a variety of languages is simple.

Vienna welcomes you with a harmonious blend of modern conveniences and old-world charm from the moment you land by plane. The warm Austrian welcome and the airport's dedication to efficiency set the scene for the amazing experiences you will have in the center of this historically and culturally significant city. Like the city, Vienna's airport provides a lasting sense of sophistication and elegance.

By Train

Vienna has an extensive and effective rail network that connects it to other important cities in Europe. Train travel is an easy and beautiful way to get to the city. Vienna's principal train stations, Wien Hauptbahnhof (also known as Vienna principal Station) and Wien Westbahnhof (also known as Vienna West Station), serve as the city's entrances.

Wien Hauptbahnhof: The striking fusion of modern and traditional architectural features greets you as soon as you arrive at Vienna's Main Station. The station was recently expanded and underwent major renovations, making it a cutting-edge transportation hub. Its opulent exterior recalls the city's imperial past, yet the modern interior makes for a seamless welcome.

Wien Westbahnhof: Another quaint entrance is available at Vienna's West Station. It is furnished with contemporary conveniences and services without sacrificing its antique beauty. A diverse range of travel alternatives and a busy mix of passengers will be all around you.

One special benefit of traveling by rail to Vienna is that you can often get out right in the middle of the city, giving you quick access to all its historical and cultural attractions. Vienna is an ideal hub for international rail travel due to its central location in Europe.

By Car

If you would rather go by car, Vienna's vast road system makes for a convenient and easy trip. Well kept roadways encircle the city, and there is ample signage to direct you to your destination.

You may cross the famous Danube River while traveling toward Vienna, which is a wonderful way to be reminded of the city's significance in Central Europe. The famed Ringstraße, a ring road around the city, delineates Vienna's historic core. Grand boulevards, cutting-edge architectural marvels, and historic sites can all be seen as you drive through the city's well-organized streets.

In Vienna, parking is widely accessible, with many of garages and parking lots spread out over the city. Vienna's traffic laws are well-marked, and parking is a practical aspect of traveling by car, whether you want to park in a garage or on the street.

CHAPTER 2

ACCOMMODATION

5 Luxury Hotels in Vienna

Hotel Imperial: Constructed in 1863, this famous establishment is situated on Vienna's major thoroughfare, the Ringstrasse. Renowned for its lavishness and grace, it has played home to several well-known figures over the years, such as politicians, entertainers, and members of the royal family. The 138 guestrooms and suites at the hotel are all well-furnished. A spa, a fitness facility, and multiple eateries and bars are among the facilities.

Cost estimate

Nightly rate: between €400 and €1000

Suite: from €1000 to €5000 each night

Hotel Sacher: This renowned establishment is close to the Vienna State Opera on the Philharmonikerstraße. Constructed in 1876, it is renowned for both its sophisticated ambiance and its well known Sachertorte, which is a chocolate cake stuffed with apricot jam. All 99 of the hotel's rooms and suites are furnished in a traditional Viennese manner. A spa, a fitness facility, and multiple eateries and bars are among the facilities.

Cost estimate

Nightly rate: between €450 and €1100

Suite: from €1100 to €5550 per night

Hotel Bristol: Situated on Vienna's main shopping avenue, Kärntner Straße, is an opulent hotel. Constructed in 1893, it is renowned for its refined and classy ambiance. All 157 of the hotel's rooms and suites are furnished in a classic Viennese manner. A spa, a fitness facility, and multiple eateries and bars are among the facilities.

Cost estimate

Nightly rate: between €350 and €900

Suite: from €900 to €4000 each night

Palais Coburg: This luxurious hotel may be found in the heart of Vienna on the Coburgbastei, a calm street. Originally constructed in 1845, it served as the Dukes of Saxe-Coburg and Gotha's home. The hotel features sixty-four luxuriously designed rooms and suites. A spa, a fitness facility, and multiple eateries and bars are among the facilities.

Cost estimate

Nightly rate: between €500 and €1200

Suite: €12,000–$20,000 per evening

Grand Hotel Wien: This opulent establishment is situated across from the Vienna State Opera on Ringstrasse. Constructed in 1873, it is renowned for both its renowned Ring Café and its refined ambiance. All 205 of the hotel's rooms and suites are furnished in a classic Viennese manner.

A spa, a fitness facility, and multiple eateries and bars are among the facilities.

Cost estimate

Nightly rate: between €400 and €1000

Suite: from €1000 to €5000 each night

5 Low-Cost Hotels in Vienna

Do Step Inn Home - Hotel & Hostel: This lodging option is situated close to the Vienna State Opera in the center of Vienna. It provides a range of room categories, such as flats, private rooms, and dorms.

Cost estimate: Dorm beds start at €18 per night, while private rooms cost €64 per night.

Hotel Pension Arpi: This lodging option is situated in Vienna's serene Währing neighborhood. It provides a range of room categories, such as family rooms, comfort rooms, and standard rooms.

Cost estimate: Standard rooms start at €44 per night, while comfort rooms cost €65 per night.

Hotel Raimundhof: This lodging option is situated close to Kärntner Straße, a shopping avenue, in Vienna's Mariahilf neighborhood. It provides a range of room categories, such as family rooms, comfort rooms, and standard rooms.

Cost estimate: Standard rooms start at €45 per night, while comfort rooms cost €60 per night.

Hotel Graf Stadion: This lodging option is situated close to Schönbrunn Palace in Vienna's 15th district. It provides a range of room categories, such as family rooms, comfort rooms, and standard rooms.

Cost estimate: Standard rooms start at €52 per night, while comfort rooms cost €69 per night.

Ibis Budget Wien Messe: This low-cost hotel is close to the well-known Vienna Messe, a venue for trade shows and exhibitions. It provides a range of room categories, such as family rooms and basic rooms.

Cost estimate: Standard rooms start at €39 per night, while family rooms cost €59 per night.

Hostels in Vienna

Wombat's City Hostel Vienna Naschmarkt: Travelers love this contemporary, lively hostel that's close to the Naschmarkt. The hostel offers individual rooms with chic décor and spotless, roomy dorms. A vibrant bar, a shared kitchen, and a rooftop terrace with breathtaking city views are among the amenities. Due to the hostel's central position, public transportation and Vienna's attractions are easily accessible.
Cost estimate: €20–60 per night

Hostel Ruthensteiner Vienna: Hostel Ruthensteiner is a quaint, welcoming hostel housed in a 19th-century building. The hostel features dorms and individual rooms with distinctive, creative details. Regular live music events are held in the garden with a barbeque area, and there's a shared kitchen. Schönbrunn Palace is nearby, and the Westbahnhof rail station is only a short stroll away.
Cost estimate: €25–75 per night

Westend City Vienna Hostel: This is an affordable place to stay right in the middle of Vienna. Situated close to the city center and the Westbahnhof train station, it provides tidy and cozy rooms in the form of dorms. The hostel is a great starting point for seeing the sights of the city because it offers a friendly environment for those on a tight budget.

Cost estimate: €17–45 per night.

A&O Wien Stadthalle: This well-liked hostel is situated close to the Vienna Stadthalle, a sizable performance arena. A range of room types are available, such as family rooms, individual rooms, and dorms. There is also a bar, a table for pool, and table tennis at the hostel.

Cost estimate: €18–€52 per night

Staddaffe - Chic Hostel VIE: This chic hostel may be found in the Innere Stadt. A range of room types are available, such as family rooms, individual rooms, and dorms. The hostel features a common room and bar as well.

Cost estimate: €22–€62 per night

Vacation Rentals

An opulent residence within the Vienna State Opera: Situated in the center of Vienna, this opulent apartment is near the Vienna State Opera. It has a fully furnished kitchen, a large living and dining area, two bedrooms, two bathrooms, and a balcony with breathtaking city views. Modern conveniences like TV, air conditioning, washing machine, dryer, and Wi-Fi are all included in the flat.

Cost estimate: €200 per night

Währing District Family-Friendly Home: Only a short stroll from Schönbrunn Palace, this family friendly Vienna home is situated in the serene Währing neighborhood. It has a large living and dining area, a fully furnished kitchen, two bathrooms, three bedrooms, and a yard. The home is furnished with all the most modern conveniences, such as air conditioning, TV, washing machine, dryer, and Wi-Fi.

Cost estimate: €180 per night

Charming Cottage in the Vienna Woods : Only a short drive from the city center is this quaint home situated in the Vienna Woods. Along with a fully functional kitchen, a nice living room with a fireplace, a balcony with breathtaking views of the surrounding countryside, and two bedrooms, it also has one bathroom. Modern conveniences like TV, washing machine, dryer, and Wi-Fi are all included in the cottage's setup.

Cost estimate: €160 per night.

CHAPTER 3

PLANNING YOUR TRIP

Visa and Entry Requirements

For many people, visiting Vienna is their ideal trip. But it is important to know the entry and visa procedures that apply to your scenario before setting off on your adventure to this stunning European city.

Visa Exemptions: Vienna is a member of the Schengen Area, which permits travel between its member nations without the need for a visa. Citizens of the US, Canada, and Australia, as well as citizens of other Schengen member states, are not required to get a visa in order to enter Austria for short visits (up to 90 days) related to business, tourism, or family visits. You must, however, make sure your passport is still valid for at least three months after the day you plan to depart.

Visa requirements: You might need to apply for a Schengen visa before visiting Vienna if you are not a citizen of a nation that is a member of the Schengen area. The reason for your visit will determine the kind of visa you need. Applying for a business, tourist, or other type of visa like one for study or a family reunion is possible. For information on individual visa requirements, application processes, and processing timeframes, it is imperative that you get in touch with the Austrian embassy or consulate in your home nation.

Visa Application Process: The Schengen visa application process requires the following documents: a completed application form; a valid passport; evidence of travel insurance; a proof of itinerary for the entire trip; evidence of lodging in Vienna; evidence of sufficient funds to cover your stay; and, in some cases, a letter of no objection from your employer if you are traveling for work. Make sure to check with each embassy or consulate beforehand as they might have additional requirements.

Visa Fees: When requesting a Schengen visa, there are fees associated with the application process. Your age, the reason for your visit, and your nationality all affect these costs.

When applying, be careful to inquire about the current fee schedule with the appropriate Austrian authorities.

Processing Time: It is suggested to apply for your visa well in advance of the dates you intend to travel, as visa processing times can vary. Processing could take a few weeks, and it might take longer during the busiest travel times. That is why it is critical to plan appropriately.

Arriving at Vienna International Airport: Upon your arrival, you can be asked to show your valid passport, valid visa (if needed), and any supporting documentation, like your travel insurance and proof of lodging. It is vital to be truthful and ready to respond when Austrian immigration officials inquire about the reason for your travel.

Travel Insurance

Vienna, Austria, is a fascinating destination, but in order to guarantee a worry-free and seamless trip, it is imperative to think about the significance of travel insurance. When visiting Vienna, travel insurance can offer both financial security and peace of mind if unforeseen circumstances or emergencies occur. Here are some important things to think about

Medical Emergency Coverage: Although Vienna is a safe place to visit, illnesses or accidents can occur anywhere. Medical costs, such as doctor visits, hospital stays, and prescription drug costs, can be covered by travel insurance. If required, it can also help with setting up medical transportation back home.

Vacation Cancellation and Interruptions: Unexpected events like a family emergency or a sudden sickness may need you to postpone or cancel your vacation. If you must cancel your vacation or return home before your planned departure date, travel insurance can compensate you for non-refundable costs such as airfare, lodging, and tours.

Lost or Delayed Baggage: Travel insurance can pay you for necessary expenses while you wait for your things to be returned if they are lost, stolen, or delayed. In the event of loss, it may also pay for the replacement of your possessions.

Travel Delays: Unexpected events such as strikes, bad weather, or other circumstances can cause delays in your planned travels. During these delays, additional costs for lodging, food, and transportation may be covered by travel insurance.

Emergency Evacuation: Travel insurance can pay for the expense of an emergency evacuation in severe circumstances, such as natural catastrophes or political turmoil, to guarantee your safety and well being.

Personal Liability: Travel insurance can pay for your legal costs and liability in the unlikely event that you damage property or hurt someone.

Coverage for Preexisting Medical illnesses: If you meet specific requirements, such buying the insurance soon after scheduling your trip, some travel insurance policies may cover preexisting medical illnesses.

It is crucial to take your unique demands and the kinds of activities you want to do in Vienna into account when choosing a travel insurance coverage. To completely understand what is and is not covered, make sure to read the policy specifics, including coverage limitations, exclusions, and the claims procedure.

When to Visit Vienna

Vienna has a distinct appeal all year long, so the best time to visit will depend on your preferences and the kind of experience you are looking for. The ideal season to visit Vienna depends on several factors, including the weather, seasonal attractions, and cultural events. When planning a trip to Vienna, keep the following in mind

Spring (April to June)

- Vienna is most enjoyable in the spring. As the city emerges from its winter hibernation, you may see parks and gardens, like the famous Schönbrunn Palace Gardens, come to life.
- The temperature range of 50°F to 70°F (10°C to 24°C) is mild, making it the perfect weather for outdoor exploration.
- You will have the opportunity to take part in customary spring markets and festivities, like the Vienna Festival and the Easter markets.

Summertime (July to August)

- In Vienna, summer is the busiest travel season. Numerous outdoor activities, music festivals, and open-air concerts bring the city to life.

- With temperatures ranging from 70°F to 80°F (24°C to 27°C), the pleasant weather makes it possible to enjoy al fresco eating in the city's quaint cafes and leisurely strolls along the Danube River.

- But at this time, be ready for bigger crowds and more expensive prices. Reservations for lodging and tours should be made well in advance.

Fall (September to October)

- When the summer crowds start to thin out and the weather stays nice, early autumn is a great time to visit Vienna.

- The vivid hues of the fall foliage bring about a transformation in the city's parks, such as the Prater and Stadtpark.

- Enjoy the local crop at one of the many Heuriger wine bars or go to the Vienna International Film Festival.

Winter (November to February)

- Wintertime in Vienna is ideal for anyone who love the jovial holiday vibe. The charming displays of the city's Christmas markets, such those at Rathausplatz and Schönbrunn Palace, are well-known.

- Anticipate chilly weather, with highs of 30°F to 40°F (-1°C to 4°C), which is perfect for mulling wine and touring the city's palaces and museums.

- Vienna's New Year's Eve festivities, which include the world-famous New Year's Concert performed by the Vienna Philharmonic, are legendary and provide a one-of-a-kind experience.

CHAPTER 4

SIGHTSEEING AND ATTRACTIONS

Historic Sites

Hofburg Palace

One of the most famous and important historical sites in Austria is the Hofburg Palace, which is situated in the center of Vienna. The magnificent imperial palace is a reminder of the opulent past of the Habsburg dynasty, who ruled over a sizable empire for many years. The expansive Hofburg complex, which covers 13.6 acres, gives tourists a look into the luxurious past of the Austrian monarchy and its impact on European history.

Hofburg Palace's history began when it was built as a medieval castle in the thirteenth century. It underwent multiple restorations and additions over the ages, giving rise to a beautiful palace complex that is representative of several architectural eras, including Neoclassical, Gothic, Renaissance, and Baroque.

Being the former imperial palace of the Habsburgs is one of Hofburg Palace's most important characteristics. Notable monarchs including Empress Elisabeth (Sisi) and Emperor Francis Joseph I called it home; their lives and legacies are entwined with the history of the palace. The palace's numerous rooms and apartments, with their perfectly kept furniture, artwork, and décor, offer an insight into the everyday activities of these regal individuals.

One of the main attractions at Hofburg is the Imperial Apartments, which are made up of 19 state chambers that were originally used by Emperor Francis Joseph and Empress Elisabeth. It is possible for guests to tour their audience rooms, private rooms, and even Sisi's dressing room, which displays her renowned beauty and sense of style.

The Spanish Riding School, which is well-known for both its Lipizzaner stallions and the discipline of classical dressage, is another outstanding feature of Hofburg Palace. The school still hosts training sessions and performances so that guests can see the beauty and grace of these amazing horses.

Showcasing an extensive collection of porcelain and silverware used by the Habsburg court, the Imperial Silver Collection is one of the most significant features of Hofburg Palace. The collection sheds light on the imperial family's lavish partying and dining customs.

The Imperial Chapel, sometimes referred to as the Hofburg Chapel or the Burgkapelle, is another location within the Hofburg complex where the Vienna Boys' Choir has been performing for more than 500 years. Regular concerts and masses are held at this historic location, allowing guests to enjoy the heavenly music that has been resonating through the palace for decades.

In addition to being a storehouse of historical information, Hofburg Palace is essential to modern Austria. The Austrian National Library and the Austrian National Archives are among the government offices housed there, along with the Austrian President's official residence.

Schönbrunn Palace

The historic and architectural masterpiece known as Schönbrunn Palace is situated in Vienna, Austria, and serves as a testament to the rich cultural legacy and imperial splendor of the past. Offering a look into the luxurious past of the Habsburg monarchy and the splendors of the Baroque era, this UNESCO World Heritage Site is one of Vienna's most visited and famous sites.

When Emperor Leopold I gave the order to build a hunting lodge on the property in the late 17th century, Schönbrunn Palace's history began. However, the palace underwent a major transformation into the opulent home that exists today in the 18th century, under the reign of Empress Maria Theresa. The word Schönbrunn means "beautiful spring," which perfectly captures the essence of the palace's and its stunning gardens' splendor.

Exquisite features elaborate inner chambers, and a massive façade define the palace, which is a remarkable example of Baroque architecture. Exquisite state chambers such as the

Great Gallery, where Mozart once entertained the royal family, and the Hall of Mirrors, which takes its cues from the Palace of Versailles, are open for exploration by guests.

Schönbrunn Palace is renowned for its magnificent gardens, which span 1.2 square kilometers. The expertly tended lawns, elaborate fountains, statues, and well-placed flowerbeds make up the gardens, which are a masterwork of design. The Great Parterre, a tiered garden with hedgerows on either side and classical statue adorning it, is a feature.

With sweeping views of the palace and its grounds, the Gloriette is a stately building perched on a hill. Currently housing a café where guests may have meals or coffee while admiring the breathtaking views, it was formerly used as the Habsburgs' dining hall.

Schönbrunn Palace Park is a site of cultural value in addition to being a visual treat. The Neptune Fountain, the Roman Ruin, and the Privy Garden are among its highlights. Every space captures the visual and creative ideals of the era.

Situated within the palace grounds, the Tiergarten Schönbrunn is the oldest zoo in the world and one of Schönbrunn Palace's most charming attractions. The zoo was founded in the eighteenth century and provides a wide variety of animals in addition to being a center for education and conservation.

Vienna's Schönbrunn Palace is a hive of cultural activity, hosting a variety of events such as classical performances. Held in the gardens of the palace, the Vienna Philharmonic's Summer Night Concert is a well known outdoor concert.

Belvedere Palace

Vienna, Austria's Belvedere Palace complex is a magnificent architectural work of art that captures the opulence of the Baroque era. Vienna's artistic and cultural legacy is exemplified by the Upper and Lower Belvedere, two magnificent palaces set among exquisitely designed gardens that serve as a tribute to the city's imperial past.

Early in the eighteenth century, the renowned military leader and art enthusiast Prince Eugene of Savoy provided financial support for the construction of the Belvedere Palace.

Renowned Baroque architect Johann Lucas von Hildebrandt created the palace, which housed Prince Eugene's extensive art collection in addition to serving as an opulent home.

The Upper Belvedere is the complex's centerpiece and a work of architectural art, distinguished by its eye-catching façade and graceful proportions. The inside features an impressive collection of Austrian art, which includes the greatest collection of paintings by Gustav Klimt in the world, which includes the well-known piece "The Kiss." The Upper Belvedere also houses other treasures by artists like Oskar Kokoschka and Egon Schiele.

Originally intended to be a guest palace, the Lower Belvedere is a tasteful fusion of Baroque and Rococo architecture. The palace is home to a worldwide art collection with a 17th and 18th century emphasis. Especially, the Marble Hall represents Vienna's rich cultural heritage by providing a magnificent setting for events and performances.

One of the complex's highlights is the Belvedere Gardens, which feature immaculately kept lawns, reflecting pools, statues, and bubbling fountains. The garden offers a peaceful haven in the middle of the city thanks to its French formal garden design. Guests are welcome to stroll slowly along the garden paths while taking in the views of the surrounding city and the palaces.

Apart from its cultural function, the Belvedere Palace is a vibrant center for art shows, events, and musical performances. Vienna's palace is a thriving cultural hub that frequently presents temporary exhibitions including a wide variety of art and artists.

Museums and Galleries

The Kunsthistorisches Museum

The Museum of Art History, also known as the Kunsthistorisches Museum, is a veritable gold mine of art and culture situated in Vienna. Positioned on the well-known Ringstrasse, this splendid museum is well-known for its exceptional collection of great art, which spans several centuries and encompasses a wide range of styles and civilizations.

Founded in 1891, the museum is one of the most significant art museums globally, housing the extensive art collection of the Habsburg monarchy. Architect Gottfried Semper created the museum's neoclassical facade, which is a work of art in and of itself. The massive stairway that leads to the entryway and the imposing front both give away the splendors that lie within.

Visitors are treated to an astounding collection of artwork and historical objects at the Kunsthistorisches Museum. Ancient Egypt, Greece, and Rome are represented in the museum's vast collections of ornamental arts, sculptures, paintings, and antiquities. But its striking European paintings which include pieces by some of the greatest painters in art history, including Rembrandt, Vermeer, Rubens, and Titian are arguably what have made it most famous.

Pieter Bruegel the Elder's "The Tower of Babel," renowned for its profound symbolism and minute workmanship, is among the most famous paintings kept at the museum. With a variety of items that provide insight into ancient societies, the Kunsthistorisches Museum's collection of Egyptian and near eastern antiquities is another noteworthy attraction.

The museum's interior, with its lavish halls that capture the imperial splendor of the Habsburg dynasty, huge staircases, and elaborate marble and stucco decorations, is a work of art in and of itself. It is an immersive experience that takes guests to a different era and location, not merely a place to appreciate art.

Albertina Museum

Art lovers and history fans should both visit Vienna, Austria's Albertina Museum, a cultural treasure known for its outstanding collection of paintings and graphic works. Located in the center of Vienna, the Albertina is home to a grand palace that displays a collection of masterpieces from many eras and artistic movements.

The Duke Albert of Saxe-Teschen and his wife, the Archduchess Maria Christina, were known for their love of art and collecting, and the Albertina was formerly their home palace. They created one of the most important graphic arts collections in the world when they allowed the public to view their private collection of artworks in 1805. Currently, the museum is home to over a million pieces of art, including rare manuscripts, prints, drawings, and photos.

An outstanding feature of the Albertina collection is the wide range of drawings and prints by famous painters, including Gustav Klimt, Michelangelo, Albrecht Dürer, and Leonardo da Vinci. The breadth and depth of these pieces offer priceless insights into the minds of the greatest artists in history.

Apart from its collection of graphic arts, the Albertina has a wide variety of paintings, which include works by Impressionists, Expressionists, and contemporary artists. Every visit to the museum is a unique experience because of the regular special exhibitions that highlight a variety of artistic styles and movements.

A key component of the museum experience is the magnificent and ancient building of the Albertina Museum, which features tasteful staterooms, big staircases, and sumptuous furnishings. It offers a window into Vienna's splendor and refinement during the imperial era.

Beyond its cultural riches, the Albertina's magnificent terrace provides breathtaking views of the Hofburg Palace and the Vienna State Opera to its guests. Visitors can enjoy Vienna's cultural and architectural wonders from this vantage point.

Leopold Museum

The vivid world of Austrian and Central European art from the late 19th and early 20th centuries is celebrated in the Leopold Museum, a cultural treasure situated in Vienna. A remarkable treasure trove of Secessionist, Expressionist, and other modernist treasures, this museum is named for its founder, Rudolf Leopold.

Prominent artists like Richard Gerstl, Oskar Kokoschka, Gustav Klimt, and Egon Schiele have a remarkable variety of pieces in the museum's collection. During a time of significant innovation and cultural change, these artists, who were part of the Vienna Secession movement, were crucial in forming the artistic identity of the city.

Among the most important in the world, the Leopold Museum's collection of Egon Schiele's works is one of its main attractions. With his profound investigations of the human form and mind, Schiele's emotionally charged and provocative paintings and drawings never fail to enthrall and challenge spectators.

The museum's exceptional collection is appropriately complemented by its central Vienna position in the

MuseumQuartier. An enticing area to investigate the many artistic movements of the early 20th century is created by the building's architecture, which was built by Ortner & Ortner and skillfully combines history and modernity.

The Leopold Museum offers visitors new insights into this vibrant era of art history in addition to its permanent collection through special exhibitions that highlight different facets of Austrian and Central European art.

Churches and Cathedrals

St. Stephen's Cathedral

In the center of Vienna stands the famous and breathtaking St. Stephen's Cathedral, also known as Stephansdom in German. The mother church of the Vienna Roman Catholic Archdiocese, this magnificent Gothic cathedral is a representation of the city's rich spiritual, cultural, and historical legacy.

Building on the cathedral took several centuries, starting in the 12th century and ending in a beautiful fusion of Gothic,

Baroque, and Romanesque architectural styles. The South Tower, which rises to a height of 136 meters (446 feet), is its most notable feature. A visual spectacle from every viewpoint, the elaborate facade is embellished with colorful roof tiles and complex stone sculptures.

The interior of St. Stephen's Cathedral is just as remarkable, featuring a lofty nave, ceilings with rib vaults, and a multitude of chapels. Awe and devotion are evoked by the interior's grandeur, which is highlighted by its magnificent stained-glass windows and elaborate altars.

Climbing the 343 steps of the South Tower offers access to the spectacular rooftop of St. Stephen's Cathedral, one of the most cherished features of the building. Visitors can enjoy expansive views of Vienna from this location, which include the Danube River, the surrounding architecture, and the historic city center. Those that take on the challenge of reaching the top find it to be a fulfilling experience.

Residents of Vienna have a particular place in their hearts for St. Stephen's Cathedral, which is essential to the city's cultural character. A journey to St. Stephen's Cathedral in Vienna is a must, regardless of your interest in its architectural significance, historical significance, or spiritual significance.

Karlskirche

Karlskirche, or St. Charles's Church, is one of Vienna's most recognizable buildings and a magnificent example of architectural design. This majestic Baroque church, located on the city's Karlsplatz, is a testament to Austria's rich artistic and spiritual legacy.

Karlskirche's construction was commissioned to mark the conclusion of Vienna's horrific plague epidemic in 1713, and work on the building began in the early 1700s. The church's design combines a variety of architectural features, such as those from ancient Greek and Roman architecture, with the grandeur of the Baroque style to create an aesthetically remarkable and distinctive building.

Karlskirche's massive dome, which is capped by an amazing cupola and reaches at a height of 72 meters (236 feet), is one of its most prominent characteristics. The church's namesake, Saint Charles Borromeo, is a patron saint of those who suffer from the plague. Johann Michael Rottmayr painted the frescoes on the dome, which feature episodes from his life. Some of Vienna's most exquisite frescoes are thought to be these ones.

There is a big portico in front of the church, flanked by two giant sculptures and framed by massive columns. Karlskirche's interior is as stunning, including elaborate marble columns, stucco work, and richly decorated altars. The project's architect, Johann Bernhard Fischer von Erlach, created an altar for the church.

Additionally, Karlskirche provides tourists with the option to climb the dome for expansive views of Vienna. Ascending the church's spiral staircase brings you to an observation platform with breathtaking city views.

Karlskirche is not only a significant architectural landmark but also a thriving hub of spirituality and culture. It is a vibrant and active element of Vienna's cultural scene, hosting a range of events such as religious services and classical performances.

Votivkirche

Vienna, Austria is home to the spectacular neo-Gothic Votivkirche, also known as the Votive Church of St. Leopold. This remarkable architectural marvel is evidence of the Habsburg Empire's tenacity as well as a symbol of faith. As a token of appreciation for Emperor Franz Joseph I's escape from an attempted murder in 1853, work on it was started.

The Votivkirche, created by architect Heinrich von Ferstel, is distinguished by its magnificent twin spires, which rise to a height of 99 meters (325 feet), as well as its elaborate façade, which is covered with sculptures, spires, and other elaborate embellishments. The neo-Gothic architecture and grandeur of the cathedral are further enhanced by its beautiful interior design and stained-glass windows.

As one enters the Votivkirche, they are welcomed by a stunning nave that is illuminated by the warm glow of light that filters through its vibrant stained-glass windows. The interior, with its soaring columns, elaborate altars, and dexterous carvings that accentuate the neo-Gothic architectural style, exudes awe and reverence. A stunning sculpture of the Virgin Mary is located atop the high altar.

One of the most remarkable aspects of Votivkirche is its exquisite rose window, which is a magnificent example of Gothic Revival architecture and is situated above the main entrance. The church also has an amazing collection of sculptures, frescoes, and mosaics that enhance the visitor's understanding of the cathedral's spiritual and artistic value.

Vienna's Votivkirche is a landmark both historically and culturally, in addition to being a house of prayer. Its historical significance as an architectural marvel shows the continuing faith and determination of the people of Vienna and Austria as a whole. It routinely hosts concerts, events, and significant religious rituals. A peek into this fascinating city's rich history, art, and spirituality can be had by visiting the Votivkirche.

Parks and Gardens

Stadtpark

The City Park, also known as Stadtpark, is a lush haven in the center of Vienna and is frequently cited as one of the most exquisite and tranquil urban parks on the planet. This verdant and serene park offers both residents and visitors a pleasant haven where they may relax, take in the scenery, and become immersed in art and culture. It is a wonderful diversion from the busy metropolis.

Stadtpark was one of Vienna's first public parks, established in the middle of the 1800s. The park's design blends romantic movement inspired ornamental and decorative elements with English landscape garden design components.

A defining characteristic of Stadtpark is the golden statue of Johann Strauss II, the well-known Austrian musician popularly referred to as the "Waltz King." Recalling Strauss's contributions to the field of classical music, this statue is a cherished representation of Vienna's musical past.

A peaceful natural backdrop that encourages exploration and relaxation is created by the park's numerous walking routes, winding streams, and little bridges. The well designed gardens and surrounding scenery make it a well-liked location for leisurely walks, picnics, and relaxation.

Stadtpark is a center for art and culture in addition to being a beautiful natural setting. It is an active hub for expression and creativity since it holds a range of activities, such as outdoor concerts, art exhibits, and cultural festivals. The park is a must-visit location for anyone looking for a quiet and cultural getaway in Vienna because of its historical significance, artistic components, and tranquil ambiance.

Prater Park

Vienna's Prater Park, also known as the Prater, is a widely recognized public park and entertainment center. This expansive green haven is a favorite spot for both locals and visitors, providing a beautiful blend of natural beauty, family-friendly entertainment, and a hint of history.

The Prater's history began in the sixteenth century, when the Habsburg family utilized it as a hunting area. After being eventually made public in the late 1700s, it has developed into a multipurpose area for pleasure.

The Wiener Riesenrad, or giant ferris wheel, is one of the Prater's most iconic features. Built in 1897, this famous landmark now serves as a symbol of Vienna and provides sweeping city vistas. For tourists, riding the Ferris wheel is a must do experience since it offers a distinctive viewpoint of the city's surroundings.

The Prater is home to a variety of rides, thrill rides, bumper cars, and roller coasters in addition to the Ferris wheel. All ages can have fun and thrill at the Wurstelprater, which is made up of several attractions combined.

Past the entertainment, the Prater offers large open areas, trails for bicyclists and walkers, and shady spots ideal for picnics. The expansive meadows in the park are perfect for leisurely strolls and outdoor pursuits.

The Hauptallee, a broad avenue lined with trees that winds through the Prater and offers a picturesque path for bikers, joggers, and leisurely strollers, is one of the park's most appealing features.

Volksgarten

The magnificent and historically significant Volksgarten, often known as the People's Garden, is in the center of Vienna. Renowned for its exquisite architecture, breathtaking rose gardens, and its significance in conserving the city's legacy, this charming green area is well-known.

The Volksgarten's history dates to the early 1800s, when Emperor Franz I established it as a part of his plan to improve Vienna's aesthetic appeal and livability. The park, which is close to the Hofburg Imperial Palace, features traditional patterns mixed with lush flora in a harmonic blend of French and English landscape styles.

The assortment of rose gardens at Volksgarten is among its most alluring characteristics. With over 3,000 rose bushes that blossom in a magnificent array of hues and fragrances throughout the summer, the Volksgarten Rose Garden is a sight to behold. Explore a wide variety of rose varietals and enjoy their fragrances and beauty.

The Theseus Temple, a graceful Neoclassical building with a sculpture of the mythological hero Theseus battling the Minotaur, is another reason for Volksgarten's notoriety. This temple offers a beautiful setting for strolls and is a well-liked location to enjoy the tranquil atmosphere of the park.

The park's winding paths, which are shaded by tall trees, provide a tranquil haven from the busy metropolis and a welcoming environment for leisurely strolls, picnics, and relaxation. Both locals and guests will find refuge in the peaceful ambiance and soft sounds of the fountains.

The historical significance of Volksgarten goes beyond its verdant surroundings. Vienna's architectural legacy is preserved in part by the park that sits next to the Hofburg Palace. The park's cultural and historical appeal is enhanced by a multitude of monuments, such as the Empress Elizabeth Monument, which honors the adored Empress Sisi, in addition to the Theseus Temple.

The Vienna State Opera

One of the most renowned and esteemed opera venues in the world is the Vienna State Opera, or Wiener Staatsoper in German. This cultural landmark is widely associated with the city's musical legacy, rich history, and unwavering commitment to the performing arts.

Originally known as the Vienna Court Opera, the Vienna State Opera began its existence in the 19th century. Architects August Sicard von Sicardsburg and Eduard van der Null created a masterpiece in the current neoclassical edifice, which first opened its doors in 1869. This architectural marvel, which captures the opulence and creative goals of the Habsburg monarchy, is a monument to Vienna's imperial past.

The repertory of the opera house is equally spectacular, encompassing a wide variety of ballets and operas that are performed in a variety of genres, from classical to modern. Its stage has featured the creations of famous composers like Richard Strauss, Johann Strauss II, and Wolfgang Amadeus Mozart. The annual Vienna Opera Ball, a beautiful and legendary event that embodies the city's legacy of elegance and sophistication, is the reason behind the Vienna State Opera's fame.

The Vienna State Opera's group of elite singers, conductors, and musicians is one of its most treasured traditions. The opera building frequently hosts performances by the internationally acclaimed Vienna Philharmonic, an orchestra with a rich history. The prestigious Vienna State Ballet enhances the institution's appeal with its well-known performers and choreographers.

The Vienna State Opera is a representation of Vienna's cultural identity in addition to being a center of creative excellence. Its ongoing significance and influence on the international opera and ballet scenes are guaranteed by its dedication to presenting both classic and contemporary works as well as to developing up-and-coming artists.

Its lavish décor, with its elaborate chandeliers and decorations, makes for an enchanted experience for guests of the opera house. In addition to being a work of architectural art, it offers guided tours that let guests discover its rich past and enduring beauty outside of the performances.

CHAPTER 5

TRANSPORTATION AND GETTING AROUND

Train and Bus Transportation

Trains, buses and trams are all part of Vienna's extensive public transit network. Wiener Linien, which provides a range of tickets and passes to suit your needs, runs the city's public transit system.

Transportation by Train: The S-Bahn (suburban railway), regional trains, and U-Bahn (metropolitan train) are all part of Vienna's extensive train network. The most practical and swiftest way to move around the city core is via the U-Bahn. All of Vienna's main attractions are covered by its five lines. The city core is connected to the surrounding towns and suburbs by the S-Bahn. Vienna and other important cities in Austria and Europe are connected by regional trains.

Bus Transport Services: The entire city of Vienna is serviced by an extensive bus network. If you want to travel to and from locations not served by the U-Bahn or S-Bahn, buses are a great alternative. Additionally, there are numerous night buses that travel the entire city.

Estimated Fares: The type of ticket you buy and the number of zones you ride through determine how much the public transportation in Vienna costs. A single ticket may be purchased for €2.40 and allows for one hour of travel within the same zone. Additionally, passes for one day cost €5.80, 48 hours €14.10, or 72 hours €17.10 can be bought. A weekly or monthly pass might be something you want to think about getting if you intend to use public transit frequently.

How to Obtain Tickets: Vienna's public transport tickets can be bought at vending machines at every U-Bahn and S-Bahn station, as well as from numerous newsstands and tobacco shops. Additionally, you can buy tickets via the Wiener Linien mobile app or online.

Taxis

While taxis are a practical means of transportation in Vienna, their cost can sometimes surpass that of public transport. You can hail a taxi on the street, order one over the phone, or order one online. Taxis are accessible 24 hours a day, 7 days a week.

Taxi Fares: Government regulations govern taxi fares in Vienna, which are determined by a taximeter. A cab trip costs €4.00 at base fare. A per-kilometer fee of €1.05–€1.08 during the day and €1.18–€1.28 at night is additionally applicable. An additional cost of €27.80 per hour is associated with waiting times.

Added Fees: It is possible that your taxi fare will include a few extra fees. A few of these fees are:
- €0.30 per piece of luggage is the luggage surcharge.
- 20% more is charged for rides between 10 p.m. and 6 a.m. on weekends.
- 20% additional cost applies to rides on holidays.

Payment for Ride: A credit card or cash can be used to pay for a cab ride in Vienna. Although most cabs take major payment cards, it is usually a good idea to confirm with the driver before you begin your trip.

Recommendations for Vienna Taxi Use

- Approximately €35–€55 from the airport to the city center
- The Schönbrunn Palace is around €10–€12 from the city center.
- The Vienna State Opera is €5 to €7 from the city center.
- The city center to St Stephen's Cathedral Cost from €3 and €5

Remember that the real fee may differ based on traffic circumstances and other factors. These are only estimates.

Cycling

Riding a bicycle is a popular and eco-friendly method to get around the beautiful city of Vienna. Bike friendly rules and well planned infrastructure make Vienna a great place for cyclists to explore the city at their own leisure.

Cycle trails: Vienna has a vast network of bike lanes and trails that are specifically designed to provide safety and convenience for cyclists. These trails wind across the city, taking beautiful paths through parks, beside the Danube River, and into the old city center.

City Bike Rental: Vienna's City bike program offers both residents and tourists an easy and reasonably priced way to rent bicycles. Bicycles can be picked up and dropped off at several stations located across the city. It's a wonderful way to have a leisurely ride and see the sights of Vienna.

Scenic Routes: Prater Park offers a pleasant, car-free cycling experience, and the Danube Island (Donauinsel) has lovely bike pathways. In addition, more experienced cyclists can find demanding routes in the Vienna Woods (Wienerwald), which are located outside of the city.

Bicycle-Friendly Public Transportation: You can ride your bicycle on trams, buses, and suburban trains in Vienna's bike-friendly public transportation system.

Ridesharing

Ridesharing services such as Uber are becoming increasingly popular and practical ways to get about Vienna.. It is simple to navigate around the city when visitors and locals utilize ridesharing applications to schedule a ride. Benefits from these services include cashless transactions, transparent pricing, and driver location tracking. They enhance Vienna's public transit network and offer a substitute for conventional taxis. For safety and dependability, it is crucial to confirm that the service provider has a license and complies with local laws. With its flexibility and accessibility for both visitors and locals, ridesharing has grown to be an essential component of Vienna's urban mobility.

CHAPTER 6

DAY TRIPS FROM VIENNA

Wachau Valley

The Wachau Valley, one of Europe's most beautiful river valleys, is a charming and alluring area that is located along the Danube River in Lower Austria. It was named a UNESCO World Heritage Site because of its breathtaking natural scenery, ancient cities, and hillsides covered with vineyards.

The magnificent and varied scenery of the Wachau Valley is widely renowned. You will see beautiful vineyards, terraced slopes, quaint villages, and old castles situated on hilltops as you cruise or drive down the river. One of the most recognizable sites in the area is the spectacular Baroque monastery overlooking the river, known as the Melk Abbey.

The valley is also known for producing wine, especially Riesling and Grüner Veltliner. The remarkable quality of the area wines is attributed to their distinct terroir and mild environment. Visitors can take a tour of the wineries, sample the wines, and discover the generations old wine making customs.

It is fun to explore the Wachau Valley's charming towns, such Dürnstein and Krems. A peek of the rich history and culture of the area can be found in the cobblestone streets, old buildings, and friendly atmosphere.

Salzburg

Vienna is only a few hours' drive away from Salzburg, Austria, a cultural gem known as the "City of Mozart" and renowned for its breathtaking mountain environs. The city has gained recognition for its contributions to classical music, rich history, and stunning architecture.

Featuring a magnificently preserved medieval core with Baroque and Gothic architecture, quaint cobblestone lanes, and scenic squares, Salzburg's Old Town is a UNESCO World Heritage Site. Located on a hill with sweeping views of the city below, the Hohensalzburg Fortress provides insight into the city's military and historical significance.

Wolfgang Amadeus Mozart, the brilliant composer who was born in Salzburg in 1756, is among the most famous people connected to the city. Now a museum, his birthplace allows visitors to dive into his remarkable contributions to classical music, as well as learn about his early life and musical instruments.

International audiences and elite performers flock to the city each year for the Salzburg Festival, one of the most recognized classical music and theatrical festivals in the world. Salzburg's unwavering passion for the arts is demonstrated by this.

Salzburg provides chances for outdoor pursuits like hiking, skiing, and touring the stunning Lake District amidst its charming alpine backdrop. The city's Salzach River meanders through it, offering lovely routes for leisurely strolls.

Bratislava

The historic and quaint city of Bratislava, the capital of Slovakia, is conveniently close to Vienna, Austria. Bratislava, which lies on the banks of the Danube River, is a location rich in history, culture, and breathtaking architecture that is also easily accessible as a day trip from Vienna.

The medieval castle in Bratislava, called Bratislavský hrad, is one of the city's most recognizable features. The castle, which is perched on a hilltop overlooking the city, is a well-liked tourist destination because it provides expansive views of the surroundings, including Vienna. Bratislava's Old Town is a charming neighborhood with meandering, narrow streets, vibrant baroque buildings, and a bustling vibe. Historic sites, quaint cafés, and cultural events all congregate in the Main Square.

Bratislava is renowned for its active eating scene and café culture as well. In the city's quaint cafés and restaurants, guests can enjoy a cup of coffee or a glass of local wine while indulging in traditional Slovak cuisine.

The magnificent Gothic building known as St. Martin's Cathedral, which has an amazing steeple, is one of the highlights of a trip to Bratislava. Slovakia's history and culture can be learned about from the many museums in the city, such as the Slovak National Museum and the Museum of Transport.

For visitors to the Austrian capital, Bratislava is an easy and educational day excursion because of its proximity to Vienna. Bratislava offers a singular and satisfying experience, regardless of your interests in history, culture, or just touring a quaint European city.

CHAPTER 7

NIGHTLIFE AND ENTERTAINMENT

Nightclubs and Bar

Vienna is renowned for its classical music and artwork, but it is also known for its exciting nightlife, with a wide range of pubs and clubs to suit every taste. These places give both locals and guests the chance to relax, mingle, and dance the night away.

Different musical genres and atmospherics can be found in Vienna's nightclubs. The city's techno culture is especially vibrant, with well-known DJs and events held at locations like Pratersauna and Grelle Forelle. Another legendary nightclub, Flex, is situated beneath the Danube Canal's arches and is known for its wide selection of music.

The Albertina Passage offers a unique and sophisticated combination of great cuisine, music and art, perfect for those seeking a touch of luxury and classical Viennese elegance.

The Volksgarten Pavillon, situated in the historic Volksgarten Park, is a stylish outdoor space ideal for conversation and beverages for those looking for a more private experience.

There are many kinds of bars in Vienna, ranging from classy cocktail clubs to quaint neighborhood spots. Known for its excellent cocktails, the ageless classic Loos American Bar bears the name of its architect, Adolf Loos. The top level of the Sofitel Vienna has a bar called Das Loft, which offers stunning views of the city skyline for a more contemporary experience.

A special ambiance is created for having an after-dinner drink and dessert at places like Café Schwarzenberg and Café Sacher, which are part of the city's ancient café culture that continues into the evening.

Even if Vienna's nightlife isn't as widely recognized as its daytime cultural attractions, it's nonetheless vibrant and offers something for every taste and preference. If you're looking for a classic Viennese café, an underground party, or an upscale cocktail lounge, Vienna has something to offer everyone when it comes to nightlife.

Vienna's Classical Music Legacy

Vienna's legacy in classical music is evidence of the city's lasting dedication to fostering musical talent as well as its significant effect on the music industry. The capital of Austria has served as a creative hotbed, giving birth to some of the most well known composers and performers in history, and it continues to be a major hub for classical music worldwide.

The Austrian Habsburg monarchy, which attracted and fostered many gifted musicians and composers, is strongly associated with Vienna's rich musical history. Some of the greatest names in classical music history, including Wolfgang Amadeus Mozart, Ludwig van Beethoven, Joseph Haydn, and Franz Schubert, were born and raised in Vienna. Among the historical sites honoring their legacy are Mozart's apartment, Beethoven's Heiligenstadt Testament, and Haydn's last resting place.

One of the most renowned orchestras in the world and a symbol of Vienna's superiority in music is the Vienna Philharmonic Orchestra, which was established in 1842. It has graced grand venues all throughout the world and still draws the best performers.

Vienna's architectural wonders, the state opera house and Musikverein, as well as other music halls and opera houses, are home to world class performances all year long. A cultural highlight that honors the city's musical legacy is the Vienna Philharmonic's yearly New Year's Concert, which is televised to millions of people worldwide.

Vienna's thriving performance scene and extensive history of music education guarantee that classical music will always be very much in the city. The University of Music and Performing Arts Vienna attracts students from all over the world, which contributes to the city's rich musical history.

CHAPTER 8

CUISINE AND DINING

Traditional Austrian Dishes

Austria's rich culinary legacy is reflected in its exquisite traditional food. Austrian cuisine is renowned for its robust and vibrant taste, drawing inspiration from diverse geographical areas. The Wiener Schnitzel, a breaded and deep-fried cutlet of veal or pork, is a famous delicacy that is typically paired with sweet lingonberry jam and tart lemon.

The iconic Apfelstrudel, a delicious pastry filled with spiced apples, and the Sachertorte, an opulent chocolate cake decorated with apricot jam, are two examples of Austria's dessert obsession.

Warming the soul is goulash, a hearty stew with tender bits of meat and paprika; for a more sophisticated meal, try Tafelspitz, which is slow-cooked boiling beef served with a rich broth and traditional sides.

Comforting classics like fluffy pancakes Kaiserschmarrn and cheese dumplings Kasnocken are other features of Austrian cuisine. Beyond the traditional fare, the nation's culinary diversity is exhibited by regional delicacies including potato salad and meatloaf, or Leberkäse. The flavors of Austrian food are celebrated, together with tradition and a kind demeanor that invites all to the table.

Viennese Coffee Culture

Vienna's beloved coffee traditions are an essential component of the city's social fabric and go beyond simple coffee-drinking customs. Coffee shops in Vienna have been important centers of learning and culture since the 17th century. They create a special environment that is just as much about relaxing and discussion as it is about the coffee.

More important than the coffee itself, the typical Viennese coffeehouse experience is about living in the moment. Formal-dressed waiters provide a variety of coffee specialties, including the Melange, which is a cappuccino-like drink, Einspänner, which is espresso paired with whipped cream, and the well-known Viennese coffee. Apfelstrudel, Sachertorte, and exquisite cookies are just a few of the mouthwatering pastries that are typically served with them.

Newspapers, chess tables, and a welcoming atmosphere that invites customers to stay for hours to converse intellectually or just people watch are further characteristics of Viennese coffeehouses. These coffeehouses have added cultural significance due to their past patronage by numerous well-known artists and intellectuals, including Freud and Kafka.

A space for reflection, conversation, and cultural enrichment, the coffee shop offers more than just a location to get your caffeine fix. Vienna has a rich history and is dedicated to preserving the art of enjoying life's small pleasures, like a good cup of coffee. The city's coffeehouses have become legendary, and their legacy lives on.

CHAPTER 9

SHOPPING IN VIENNA

Luxury Boutiques

Luxury boutiques in Vienna live up to the city's reputation for grandeur and elegance. Vienna has everything to offer even the pickiest consumer, from exclusive jewelry retailers to internationally recognized fashion firms.

The following list of Vienna's most opulent stores includes an estimate of costs:

Chanel: Every luxury shopper should make time to visit Chanel, the renowned French design brand. Chanel's Vienna store, which provides a large selection of apparel, accessories, and handbags, is situated on the upscale Kohlmarkt retail district. Chanel handbags range in price from approximately 500 euros to tens of thousands of euros, with evening gowns and fur coats being the most expensive products.

Hermès: Another prestigious fashion brand, Hermès is well-known for its fine leather products. A large selection of purses, wallets, belts, and other leather items are available at the Hermès Vienna boutique, which is situated in the Graben retail district. Hermès wallets range in price from approximately €1,000 to tens of thousands of euros, with high-end pieces like Birkin purses costing much more.

Louis Vuitton: The French luxury company Louis Vuitton is recognized for its ready-to-wear apparel, luggage, and handbags with monograms. Situated on Kärntner Straße, the luxury retail avenue, the Louis Vuitton Vienna boutique has an extensive selection of items for both genders. Louis Vuitton handbags start at about €500, while high-end pieces like luggage sets can cost up to tens of thousands of euros.

Cartier: One of the most renowned watch and jewelry manufacturers in the world is Cartier, a French company. For both men and women, the Cartier Vienna store is situated on the Kohlmarkt retail district and provides an extensive selection of jewelry, watches, and accessories. For a little piece of jewelry, prices for Cartier start about €500. For high-end products like diamond necklaces and watches, prices can reach hundreds of thousands of euros.

Tiffany & Co: This American merchant of fine jewelry and silverware is recognized for its engagement rings and other exquisite pieces. The Kohlmarkt retail district is home to the Tiffany & Co. Vienna boutique, which sells a large selection of watches, jewelry, and silverware for both men and women. A little piece of jewelry from Tiffany & Co. can cost as little as €500, while high-end pieces like diamond engagement rings can cost as much as hundreds of thousands of euros.

Souvenirs

Here are some of the most common souvenirs from Vienna, along with an approximate price:

Mozartkugeln: Among the most recognizable takeaways from Vienna are these balls made of chocolate and marzipan. They are named for the famous Austrian composer Wolfgang Amadeus Mozart and are available in dark chocolate, pistachio, and hazelnut tastes. A modest box of Mozartkugeln normally costs about €10.

Sachertorte: Another well-liked memento from Vienna is this chocolate cake with apricot jam inside. Franz Sacher, the son of the Austrian emperor's chef, invented it in the 19th century. Vanilla ice cream or whipped cream are common toppings for Sachertorte. While individual slices from various bakeries and cafes can be had for about €5, a whole Sachertorte from the Hotel Sacher can set you back about €40.

Vienna snow globes: A timeless memento that is sure to please are Vienna snow globes. They are made in many different sizes and forms, and they frequently include well-known Vienna sights like Schönbrunn Palace and St. Stephen's Cathedral. Vienna snow globes range in price from €10 to €20, depending on their complexity and size.

Viennese coffee: Vienna is famous for its coffee culture, so it should come as no surprise that coffee is a favorite memento to bring home. You can buy ground coffee or Viennese coffee beans, as well as a coffee machine and other supplies for making coffee. The price of 250 grams of Viennese coffee beans is normally about €10, whereas the price of ground coffee is about €5. Prices for coffee makers and related brewing supplies can range from €20 to €100 or more.

Viennese wine: Vienna is renowned for producing its own wine, so make sure to purchase a bottle to bring back home. You are sure to find a Viennese wine that appeals to you among the many varieties that are available. A bottle of Viennese wine usually costs about €10.

Viennese Porcelain: Vienna is renowned for producing superior porcelain. Vases, bowls, and figurines made of Viennese porcelain are available for purchase. Vases and dishes usually cost between €10 and €20 per piece, although figures made of Viennese porcelain can cost as much as €100 or more.

Viennese crystal: Vienna is also renowned for producing superior crystal. Vases, bowls, and glasses made with Viennese crystal are available for purchase. Vases and bowls can cost as much as €20–50, while Viennese crystal glasses are usually priced between €10–20 per piece.

Viennese handicrafts: Vienna's handicrafts have a long history of master craftsmanship. Viennese handicrafts including glassblowing, needlework, and wooden sculptures are available for purchase. The cost of a piece of Viennese craftsmanship might vary from €5 to €50 or more, based on its size and type.

Viennese cuisine: Apart from consumable mementos like Mozartkugeln and Sachertorte, you may buy other take-home treats like Manner wafers, pumpkin seed oil, and apricot jam. Pumpkin seed oil normally costs about €5 per small bottle, while Manner wafers typically cost about €2 per pack. A jar of apricot jam typically costs €3.

Vintage and Antiques

These vintage and antique locations in Vienna are listed with an approximate price

Dorotheum: Established in 1707, Dorotheum stands as one of the most distinguished and ancient auction houses globally. It has weekly auctions including a large selection of vintage and antique goods, such as silverware, jewelry, artworks, and furniture. Depending on the object, prices might vary from a few hundred to tens of thousands of euros.

Flohmarkt am Naschmarkt: Every Saturday, the Naschmarkt, a well liked outdoor market in Vienna, hosts the Flohmarkt am Naschmarkt flea market. You can find a wide range of vintage goods there, such as furniture, accessories, and clothes. Most products are priced at less than €100, which is generally extremely reasonable.

Antiquitätenzentrum Währing: The Währing neighborhood of Vienna is home to the Antiquitätenzentrum Währing. Numerous antique dealers may be found there offering a broad selection of goods, such as jewelry, paintings, and furniture. Depending on the object, prices might vary from a few hundred to tens of thousands of euros.

Vintage Kilo Sale: This Wiener Neubau neighborhood is home to this vintage apparel retailer. Prices for vintage apparel start at €15 per kilogram. Sales are made by weight. It is a terrific location to find distinctive vintage apparel at reasonable prices.

Retro Galerie: This antique furniture shop may be found in Vienna's Mariahilf neighborhood. It offers a range of antique furniture for sale, such as tables, chairs, and sofas. Depending on the object, prices might vary from a few hundred to thousands of euros.

Street Food and Markets

Vienna's lively food culture and diverse gastronomic offerings may be enjoyed through its bustling markets and street food scene. Here is a taste of what to expect from Vienna's street cuisine and markets

Naschmarkt: Situated close to the city center, the Naschmarkt is one of Vienna's most well known and expansive outdoor markets. With a huge selection of fresh vegetables, spices, cheeses, and international cuisine, it is a food lover's dream come true. You may find a wide variety of foods in the market, including Middle Eastern, Asian, and Mediterranean cuisine as well as delicacies from Vienna. Try some sushi, kebabs, falafel, and a variety of pastries. It is the ideal place to sample and explore a vast array of flavors.

Karmelitermarkt: This smaller, quaint market is situated in the second district. Locals love it for its fresh produce, handmade cheeses, and organic products. Additionally, there are booths offering specialty coffee, soups, and sandwiches. It is a nice spot to grab ingredients for a picnic at the nearby Augarten park, or to have a leisurely lunch.

Brunnenmarkt: The longest street market in Vienna is in the 16th district. A large variety of fresh fruits, vegetables, spices, and street cuisine from around the world are available at this multicultural market. It's a great place to sample new foods and discover different international cuisines.

Kutschkermarkt: Tucked away in the 18th district, this quainter little market embodies the spirit of Viennese culture. Along with fresh food and flowers, you may enjoy coffee, sandwiches, and pastries made in Austria.

Food Trucks: Vienna has welcomed the trend of food trucks by offering a variety of food trucks that are on wheels. Food trucks are commonplace at festivals, markets, and street corners, serving a variety of menu items like tacos, gourmet burgers, and vegetarian cuisine.

Würstelstände: Vienna is home to the recognizable sausage stands, or "Würstelstände," which are dispersed over the city.

They provide a selection of sausages, one of which is the well-known "Käsekrainer," a sausage stuffed with cheese. Savor a mouthwatering sausage that comes with fresh bread and mustard.

Vienna's markets and street food offer a window into the cosmopolitan character of the city in addition to giving visitors the chance to sample a variety of cuisines. Here, both locals and tourists can experience Vienna's dynamic and always-changing culinary scene while savoring delicacies from throughout the globe.

CHAPTER 10

SUGGESTIONS ON ITINERARY

5 Days Itinerary

You may take in its renowned coffeehouse culture, world-class museums, lively districts, and magnificent palaces over a five-day trip. To help you make the most of your time, consider the following itinerary

Day 1: Overview of Vienna

- **Morning:** One of Vienna's most recognizable sites, the historic St. Stephen's Cathedral, is the starting point of your tour. To see the entire vista, climb the tower.
- **Lunch:** Enjoy a leisurely meal at a classic Viennese café.
- **Afternoon:** Take a tour of the former imperial residence, Hofburg Palace, and pay a visit to the Sisi Museum. Take a stroll in the adjacent Volksgarten.

Evening: Savor a traditional meal in the center of Vienna's historic district.

Day 2: History and Art

- **Morning:** Visit the Kunsthistorisches Museum which is well-known for its art collections. Don't overlook Vienna's magnificent Kunstkammer.

- **Lunch:** Have a meal at one of the eateries within the museum.

- **Afternoon:** Take a quick stroll to the Museumquartier, where you may visit MUMOK and the Leopold Museum to view modern and contemporary art.

- **Evening:** Savor a delicious meal at one of Vienna's fine dining establishments.

Day 3: Gardens and Schönbrunn Palace

- **Morning:** Take in the stunning Schönbrunn Palace, a UNESCO World Heritage site, in the morning. Take a tour of the state rooms and meander among the vast gardens.
- **Lunch:** Have a quick meal at one of the Schönbrunn complex's cafés.
- **Afternoon:** Explore the Schönbrunn Zoo which is housed on the grounds of the palace and is the oldest zoo in the world.
- **Evening:** Head back to the city center and have dinner at a restaurant with a great view of the Danube Canal.

Day 4: Visit to Vienna Woods for the Day

- **Morning:** Spend the day exploring nature and hiking in the Vienna Woods (Wienerwald).
- **Lunch:** In a classic Heuriger, a wine tavern, savor delicacies from Austria.

- **Afternoon:** Take a trip to the quaint village of Mödling or spend some time exploring the Vienna Woods' hiking paths and vineyards.
- **Evening:** Go back to Vienna and relax in one of the city's charming wine bars.

Day 5: Belvedere Palace Visit and Farewell
- **Morning:** Take a tour of the Belvedere Palace complex, which has exquisite gardens and a collection of art.
- **Lunch:** Enjoy your meal in Belvedere, a quaint neighborhood well-known for its independent eateries and cafes.
- **Afternoon:** Explore one of Vienna's cultural institutions or take a leisurely stroll through the city's historic center for some last-minute souvenir buying, depending on when you are leaving.
- **Evening:** Take off from Vienna, packing your memories of an amazing five days spent exploring this amazing city.

7 Days Itinerary

With a 7-day itinerary, you can explore Vienna's rich history, culture, and culinary offerings while getting a deep dive into the city's center. Here's a detailed itinerary to help you get the most of Vienna throughout your week

Day 1: Historic City Center

- Commence your tour at St. Stephen's Cathedral and ascend its tower to enjoy breathtaking views of the city.
- Wander through the shopping districts of Graben and Kohlmarkt as you explore the historic core.
- Explore the Hofburg Palace, which is home to the Spanish Riding School, the Imperial Apartments, and more.
- Take in an evening classical music at the Vienna State Opera.

Day 2: Palaces and Art

- Start the day in the Kunsthistorisches Museum, which has a sizable collection of artwork from Europe.
- Explore Belvedere Palace, renowned for its Baroque architecture and art collection, in the afternoon.

- Enjoy the vistas as you stroll around the exquisite castle gardens.
- Enjoy a meal at one of the hip eateries in the Naschmarkt neighborhood throughout the evening.

Day 3: Naschmarkt and Modern Vienna

- Explore the MuseumsQuartier, which is home to organizations that promote modern art.
- Enjoy lunch at the bustling Naschmarkt food market.
- Explore the Secession Building, which is well-known for its unusual golden dome.
- Savor a fine dining experience at one of Vienna's best restaurants.

Day 4: Schönbrunn Palace

- Spend a day touring the magnificent palace and its breathtaking gardens at Schönbrunn Palace.
- For stunning views of the city and palace, visit the Gloriette.
- Discover the Schönbrunn Zoo, one of the most exquisite and historic zoos in the world.
- Go back to Vienna and have dinner in a neighborhood wine bar or cafe.

Day 5: Wachau Valley Day Trip

- Take a day excursion to the quaint Wachau Valley. Take a cruise on the Danube River.
- See the magnificent baroque masterpiece Melk Abbey.

- Discover Dürnstein, a quaint village renowned for its medieval castle and vineyards.
- In the evening, head back to Vienna and eat dinner at a neighborhood tavern.

Day 6: Vienna's Musical Heritage

- Start at the interactive exhibition of Vienna's musical history, Haus der Musik.

- Visit Wolfgang Amadeus Mozart's former home, Mozarthaus Vienna.

- Take a guided tour of the Vienna State Opera House.

- Attend a concert at one of Vienna's well-known music venues to round off your day.

Day 7: Exploration Day

- To learn about the Habsburg dynasty, begin in the Kaisergruft, the Imperial Burial Vault.

- Discover Vienna's most exquisite baroque park, Augarten.

- Experience the giant ferris wheel (Riesenrad) at Prater Park.

- In the Vienna Woods, end your week with a traditional Viennese supper at a Heuriger, a rustic wine bar.

CHAPTER 11

PRACTICAL INFORMATION

Tourist Information Centers

To help tourists make the most of their time in the Austrian capital, Vienna has a wide network of tourist information centers. These facilities offer helpful information, advice, and services to make it easier for visitors to explore the city.

Vienna Tourist Information Centers: These centers provide maps, brochures, and professional guidance and are situated at the Vienna State Opera, Albertina, and Vienna International Airport. For detailed information about sightseeing, events, and services, the central office, which is next to the State Opera, is an excellent resource.

Vienna Tourism Board: This official website is a great place to find out information on traveling to Vienna. By offering details on lodging, events, sights, and guided tours, it enables travelers to make travel plans ahead of time.

Mobile apps: For travelers, the "Vienna PASS" and "Vienna City Card" apps are indispensable. They provide details on discounts, attractions, public transit, and even offline maps.

Vienna Main Railway Station: This is home to i-Punkt Information & Service Point, which offers a variety of services in addition to information about Vienna. Here you may also rent bicycles, purchase tickets, and schedule trips.

Cultural and Tourist Information Centers: These can be found all around the city, especially in the Prater amusement park and the Naschmarkt. They provide resources and help related to destinations and activities.

Hotel Concierges: Most Vienna's hotels offer concierge services to help visitors with bookings, suggestions, and general city information.

These tourist information centers in Vienna serve a variety of purposes for visitors, providing not only useful advice but also a window into the historical, culinary, and cultural features of the city. With the use of these helpful tools, visitors may comfortably traverse Vienna, guaranteeing a positive and delightful stay in this magnificent European metropolis.

Emergency Contacts

It is crucial to know who to contact in case of emergency when visiting Vienna in order to protect your safety and well being. The following are crucial phone numbers and contacts to remember:

Emergency Services: Dial 112 for rapid assistance in the event of an accident, medical emergency, fire, or other potentially fatal scenario. All emergency services, including the police, ambulance, and fire departments, can be reached at this number.

Police: Call the Vienna Police at 133 to report any non-life-threatening incidents. They can help with a variety of problems, from little accidents to lost property.

Medical Emergencies: Call 144 to reach the Vienna Ambulance Service with any medical questions. Vienna boasts a first-rate healthcare system with highly qualified medical personnel.

Fire Department: To contact the Vienna Fire Department in the event of a fire or other fire-related emergency, dial 122. Poison Control: Call the Poison Information Center at +43 1 406 43 43 if you think someone may have poisoned you or if you need guidance on handling chemical-related crises.

Stolen or Lost Items: You can call the Vienna Police at 133 to report items that have been stolen or lost.

Tourist Emergency Services: +43 1 31310 87775 is the number to reach Vienna's dedicated tourist police. They can help with problems like misplaced passports or anxieties about travel because they are trained to support tourists.

Embassies and Consulates: If you run into diplomatic or legal difficulties, it is a good idea to have the contact details for your nation's embassy or consulate in Vienna.

Local Etiquette and Customs

Due to its rich cultural history, Vienna has its own set of conventions and etiquette that tourists should be aware of in order to be respectful of the community and fit in.

Salutations: Austrians are often courteous and formal. Unless asked to use their first name, shake hands firmly and greet someone by their title and last name when you meet them.

Punctuality: Timeliness is highly regarded. It is courteous to be on time for social events and appointments.

Table manners: Dining in Vienna might take place in a formal setting. You should keep your hands, not your elbows, on the table. Before beginning your meal, wait for the host or hostess to say "Guten Appetit".

Tipping: In cafes and restaurants, leaving a tip is traditional. Tipping is generally done in increments of 5 to 10% of the bill. Tipping a little bit more is appreciated in classy establishments.

Quiet Public Behavior: It is not appropriate to talk loudly or cause a nuisance in public areas, particularly when using public transit. Limit the amount of noise and discussion you make.

Queuing: Austrians are renowned for their polite and well-organized queuing. Hold off on moving forward in line until it is your turn. Courtesies and tolerance are essential.

Greetings in Shops: "Grüß Gott" (which translates to "Hello" or "God bless you") is the polite way to say hello to a shopkeeper when you walk in.

Language: Being able to say a few simple greetings or sentences in German would go a long way toward demonstrating respect for the native tongue and way of life.

Cultural Events: Formal attire is typically worn to classical music concerts and opera performances.

In addition to demonstrating respect for Vienna's traditions, adhering to these customs and manners will improve your contacts with the amiable residents and enable you to fully immerse yourself in the rich culture and history of this amazing city.

Currency and Money

The Euro (EUR) is the currency in use in Vienna. The following are some essential details regarding money and currencies in the Austrian capital:

Currency exchange: There are many currency exchange offices in Vienna, particularly in tourist destinations and at major train and airport terminals. Another convenient location to exchange money is a bank.

ATMs: Major credit and debit cards are accepted at the many ATMs located across the city. They offer a practical means of withdrawing euros, and the exchange rate is typically advantageous.

Credit Cards: Hotels, restaurants, and retail establishments in Vienna accept a variety of credit and debit cards. Although American Express and other major cards are generally accepted, Visa and MasterCard are the most widely used cards.

Cash vs. Cards: Although most places accept electronic payments, it's still a good idea to have some cash on hand, particularly for smaller transactions and traditional institutions. Cash is preferred by many small businesses, markets, and street sellers.

Language and Communication

German is the official language of Vienna. Nonetheless, you'll discover that English is extensively spoken and understood in this cosmopolitan city, particularly among the younger population and in tourist areas. English is widely spoken among Viennese, so you should have no problem conversing with them in eateries, lodgings, and tourist destinations.

As a gesture of respect for the local way of life, it's a good idea to pick up a few basic German words, but most signage, including menus and street signs, will normally be available in both English and German. Vienna is a multicultural city with a wide range of expat populations, which contributes to its linguistic diversity.

Due to Vienna's eclectic past, you may also hear languages like Turkish, Serbian, and Hungarian in addition to German and English.

Packing Tips

To make sure you're well-prepared and at ease throughout your stay, take into account Vienna's activities, culture, and temperature when packing for your vacation. Observe these packing guidelines:

Dress according to the weather: Vienna has many seasons. Bring light, breathable clothing in the summer (June to August) and warm layers (December to February) such as a nice coat, gloves, and a scarf.

Comfy shoes: Since Vienna is a walking city, sturdy, comfy shoes are a must. Bring shoes that are appropriate for walking the palaces and cobblestone streets.

Converter and adapter: Austria employs Type F and Type C electrical outlets, which are European in design. If necessary, make sure you have the appropriate voltage converter and adapter.

Rain gear and umbrella: As Vienna can get quite wet, having a small umbrella and a water-resistant jacket can come in quite handy.

Dress modestly: If your outfit is too exposing, it's a good idea to bring a scarf or shawl to cover your knees and shoulders when visiting churches and historic places.

Travel documents: Remember to include printed copies of all necessary documents, such as itinerary and hotel bookings, as well as your passport, travel insurance, and visa, if necessary.

Medication: Make sure you have a sufficient amount of prescription medication with you. Additionally useful are over-the-counter drugs and a basic first-aid kit.

Travel backpack: When traveling the city, a compact, light backpack can be helpful for carrying necessities.

Safety Tips

Tourists will usually find Vienna to be a friendly and safe city. But to guarantee a trouble-free visit, it's always a good idea to remain alert and informed of safety precautions:

Pickpocket Awareness: As in any large city, be watchful of your possessions, particularly in busy places, on public transit, and at popular tourist destinations. To protect your belongings, use an anti-theft bag or a money belt.

Public Transportation: The tram, bus, and metro systems in Vienna are safe and effective, but be mindful of your possessions when using them.

Night Safety: Vienna is known for its exciting nightlife but be cautious when exploring the city after dark. Remain in busy, well-lit locations; do not go alone in uncharted territory.

Traffic Safety: Although the traffic in Vienna is well organized, keep in mind that cars must drive on the right side of the road. When crossing the street, make sure to look both ways and only use the marked crosswalks.

Cultural Sensitivity: To prevent misunderstandings, show consideration for Vienna's customs and manners.

Legal Aspects: Comply with local ordinances, such as those prohibiting jaywalking and smoking in public areas. There may be severe consequences for infractions.

Travel Insurance: Make sure your policy covers medical emergencies, lost or stolen luggage, and trip cancellations.

CHAPTER 12

CONCLUSION

Useful Phrases

Knowing a few essential words in German can help you enjoy your vacation and demonstrate your respect for the local way of life when you visit Vienna. Even if many Viennese understand English, it can still be beneficial to try using some simple German words. Here are a few helpful terms

Hallo - Hello

Guten Morgen - Good morning

Guten Tag - Good day

Guten Abend - Good evening

Bitte - Please

Danke - Thank you

Ja - Yes

Nein - No

Entschuldigung - Excuse me

Sprechen Sie Englisch? - Do you speak English?

Wie geht es Ihnen? - How are you?

Wo ist...? - Where is...?

Wie viel kostet das? - How much does this cost?

Könnten Sie mir helfen? - Can you help me?

Wasser - Water

Essen - Food

Kaffee - Coffee

Tee - Tea

Brot - Bread

Wein - Wine

Bier - Beer

Zahlen, bitte - The bill, please

Wo ist die Toilette? - Where is the restroom?

Ich verstehe nicht - I do not understand

Können Sie das bitte wiederholen? - Can you please repeat that?

Sprechen Sie langsam, bitte - Speak slowly, please

Ich brauche Hilfe - I need help

Tut mir leid - I am sorry

Gute Reise - Have a good trip

Auf Wiedersehen - Goodbye

Maps

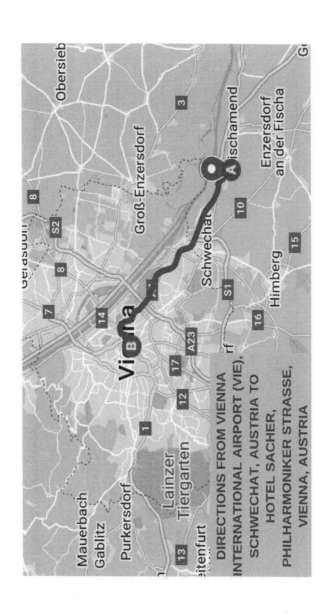

DIRECTIONS FROM VIENNA INTERNATIONAL AIRPORT (VIE), SCHWECHAT, AUSTRIA TO HOTEL SACHER, PHILHARMONIKER STRASSE, VIENNA, AUSTRIA

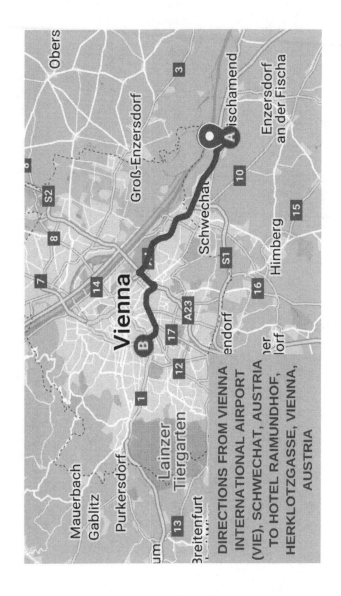

DIRECTIONS FROM VIENNA INTERNATIONAL AIRPORT (VIE), SCHWECHAT, AUSTRIA TO HOTEL RAIMUNDHOF, HERKLOTZGASSE, VIENNA, AUSTRIA

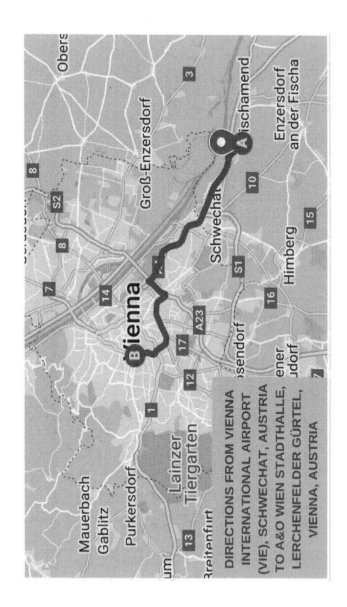

DIRECTIONS FROM VIENNA INTERNATIONAL AIRPORT (VIE), SCHWECHAT, AUSTRIA TO A&O WIEN STADTHALLE, LERCHENFELDER GÜRTEL, VIENNA, AUSTRIA

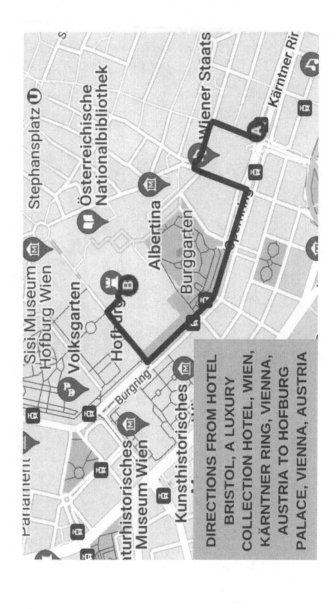

DIRECTIONS FROM HOTEL BRISTOL, A LUXURY COLLECTION HOTEL, WIEN, VIENNA, KÄRNTNER RING, VIENNA, AUSTRIA TO HOFBURG PALACE, VIENNA, AUSTRIA

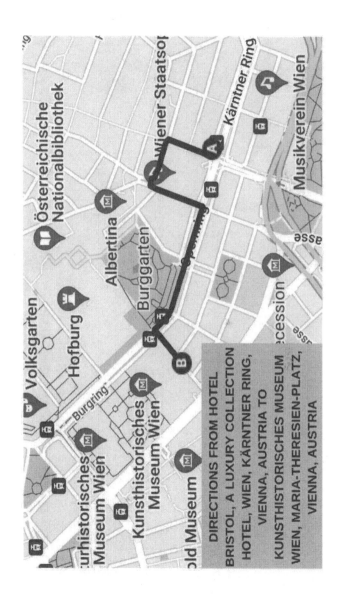

DIRECTIONS FROM HOTEL BRISTOL, A LUXURY COLLECTION HOTEL, WIEN, KÄRNTNER RING, VIENNA, AUSTRIA TO KUNSTHISTORISCHES MUSEUM WIEN, MARIA-THERESIEN-PLATZ, VIENNA, AUSTRIA

DIRECTIONS FROM HOTEL GRAF STADION, BUCHFELDGASSE, VIENNA, AUSTRIA TO KUNSTHISTORISCHES MUSEUM WIEN, MARIA-THERESIEN-PLATZ, VIENNA, AUSTRIA

DIRECTIONS FROM HOTEL GRAF STADION, BUCHFELDGASSE, VIENNA, AUSTRIA TO LEOPOLD MUSEUM, MUSEUMSPLATZ, VIENNA, AUSTRIA

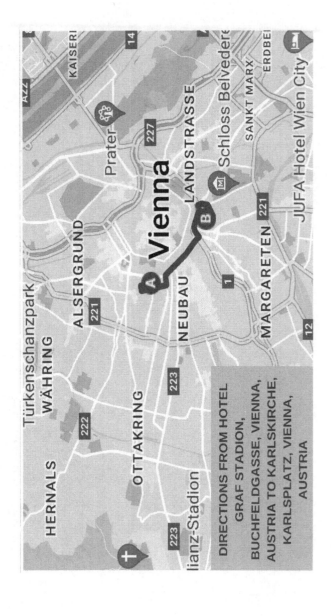

DIRECTIONS FROM HOTEL GRAF STADION, BUCHFELDGASSE, VIENNA, AUSTRIA TO KARLSKIRCHE, KARLSPLATZ, VIENNA, AUSTRIA

DIRECTIONS FROM HOTEL GRAF STADION, BUCHFELDGASSE, VIENNA, AUSTRIA TO VOLKSGARTEN, VOLKSGARTEN, HELDENPLATZ, VIENNA, AUSTRIA

141

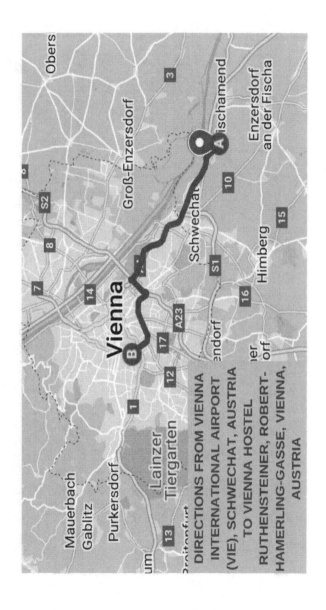

DIRECTIONS FROM VIENNA INTERNATIONAL AIRPORT (VIE), SCHWECHAT, AUSTRIA TO VIENNA HOSTEL RUTHENSTEINER, ROBERT-HAMERLING-GASSE, VIENNA, AUSTRIA

Made in the USA
Middletown, DE
03 May 2024

53840006R00082